U.S. Department of Justice

Office of Justice Programs

Office of Juvenile Justice and Delinquency Prevention

APRIL 2010

Girls
Study Group

Understanding and Responding to Girls' Delinquency

Jeff Slowikowski, Acting Administrator

Causes and Correlates of Girls' Delinquency

By Margaret A. Zahn, Robert Agnew, Diana Fishbein, Shari Miller, Donna-Marie Winn, Gayle Dakoff, Candace Kruttschnitt, Peggy Giordano, Denise C. Gottfredson, Allison A. Payne, Barry C. Feld, and Meda Chesney-Lind

According to data from the Federal Bureau of Investigation, from 1991 to 2000, arrests of girls increased more (or decreased less) than arrests of boys for most types of offenses. By 2004, girls accounted for 30 percent of all juvenile arrests. However, questions remain about whether these trends reflect an actual increase in girls' delinquency or changes in societal responses to girls' behavior. To find answers to these questions, the Office of Juvenile Justice and Delinquency Prevention convened the Girls Study Group to establish a theoretical and empirical foundation to guide the development, testing, and dissemination of strategies to reduce or prevent girls' involvement in delinquency and violence.

The Girls Study Group Series, of which this bulletin is a part, presents the Group's findings. The series examines issues such as patterns of offending among adolescents and how they differ for girls and boys; risk and protective factors associated with delinquency, including gender differences; and the causes and correlates of girls' delinquency.

Although the literature examining the causes and correlates of male delinquency is extensive, the extent to which these factors explain and predict delinquency for girls remains unclear. This bulletin summarizes results of an extensive review of more than 1,600 articles and book chapters from the social science scientific literature on individual-level risk factors for delinquency and factors related to family, peers, schools, and communities. The review, which focused on girls

ages 11 to 18, also examined whether these factors are gender neutral, gender specific, or gender sensitive.

This bulletin defines delinquency as the involvement of a child younger than 18 in behavior that violates the law. Such behavior includes violent crime, property crime, burglary, drug and alcohol abuse, and status offenses (i.e., behaviors that would not be criminal if committed by an adult) such as running away, ungovernability, truancy, and possession of alcohol.

According to arrest statistics from the Federal Bureau of Investigation, the overall rate of juvenile arrests decreased from 1994 to 2004 (Snyder, 2008). More specifically, the arrest rate for violent crimes over this period decreased 49 percent. The violent crime arrest rate then increased in 2005 by 2 percent, with a 4-percent increase in 2006. However, these overall rates obscure important variations in rates by gender. From 1997 to 2006, arrests for aggravated assaults decreased more for boys (24 percent) than for girls (10 percent). In addition, arrests for simple assault

declined by 4 percent for boys, whereas the rate for girls increased by 19 percent. Arrest data, however, are inadequate in helping to understand the factors that lead to girls' offending and arrests. To better understand the causes and correlates of girls' delinquency, this bulletin examines evidence from research studies that have explored the dynamics of girls' delinquency and risk behavior.

Data Limitations

Research indicates that risk and protective factors for delinquency may be different for boys and girls, but the mechanisms behind these differences are unclear. Delinquency research has several limitations. First, issues of selection bias when studying institutional populations have led to an increased use of cohort, neighborhood, school, and community surveys. Many of these studies rely on self-reports of delinquency by youth, who may overstate or understate delinquent behavior. On the other hand, analyses that rely on arrest data or on adult observational data typically understate the frequency of delinquent behavior. In addition, most delinquency studies are based on samples of boys, and it is unclear whether the same risk and protective factors apply equally well to girls. Much of the literature on girls' delinquency is based on small, nonrepresentative samples with few longitudinal studies or comparison groups. While recognizing these limitations, it is important to review the research to shed light on this issue and identify topics in need of further exploration.

Characteristics of Delinquent Behavior by Girls

On the whole, girls' delinquent acts are typically less chronic and often less serious than those of boys (Snyder

Girls Study Group *Members*

Dr. Stephanie R. Hawkins, Principal Investigator, Girls Study Group (April 2008–Present) Research Clinical Psychologist, RTI International

Dr. Margaret A. Zahn, Principal Investigator, Girls Study Group (2004–March 2008) Senior Research Scientist, RTI International; Professor, North Carolina State University

Dr. Robert Agnew, Professor, Department of Sociology, Emory University

Dr. Meda Chesney-Lind, Professor, Women's Studies Program, University of Hawaii–Manoa

Dr. Gayle Dakof, Associate Research Professor, Department of Epidemiology and Public Health, University of Miami

Dr. Del Elliott, Director, Center for the Study and Prevention of Violence, University of Colorado

Dr. Barry Feld, Professor, School of Law, University of Minnesota

Dr. Diana Fishbein, Director, Transdisciplinary Behavioral Science Program, RTI International

Dr. Peggy Giordano, Professor of Sociology, Center for Family and Demographic Research, Bowling Green State University

Dr. Candace Kruttschnitt, Professor, Department of Sociology, University of Toronto

Dr. Jody Miller, Associate Professor, Department of Criminology and Criminal Justice, University of Missouri–St. Louis

Dr. Merry Morash, Professor, School of Criminal Justice, Michigan State University

Dr. Darrell Steffensmeier, Professor, Department of Sociology, Pennsylvania State University

Ms. Giovanna Taormina, Executive Director, Girls Circle Association

Dr. Donna-Marie Winn, Senior Research Scientist, Center for Social Demography and Ethnography, Duke University

and Sickmund, 2006). Minor offenses predominate among female delinquent offenders.

However, minor offenses may mask serious problems that girls are experiencing. Running away from home and other status offenses (such as truancy) are major components of girls' delinquency. Studies of girls who are chronic runaways document significant levels of sexual and physical victimization (Feitel et al., 1992; Stiffman, 1989; Welsh et al., 1995). This suggests that although their offense behavior may not appear to be very serious, these girls may be fleeing from serious problems and victimization, some involving illegal behavior by adults, which in turn makes them vulnerable to subsequent victimization and engaging in other behaviors that violate the law such as prostitution, survival sex,[1] and drug use. Similarly, research on aggression in girls and assaults committed by girls suggests that these behaviors can be best understood in the context of their families, peer groups, schools, communities, and experiences (Brown, 1998; Caspi et al., 1993; Champion and Durant, 2001; Johnson, 2002; Leitz, 2003; Lockwood, 1997; Margolin and Gordis, 2000; Molnar et al., 2005; Warr, 1996).

Biological and Individual Factors

Biological Factors

Research conducted to date suggests that subtle differences in certain biological functions and psychological traits may contribute to gender-related variations in responses to certain environmental conditions (Klein and Corwin, 2002). These basic differences may, in effect, partially account for ways in which girls' delinquency is contrasted with that of boys. However, the paucity of studies specific to girls' delinquency that include biological factors precludes

any definitive conclusions at this time. One theoretical model for understanding individual-level factors in girls' delinquency proposes that although similar risk factors may play a role in both girls' and boys' delinquency, gender differences in underlying biological functions, psychological traits, and social interpretations can result in different types and rates of delinquent behaviors for girls and boys (Moffitt et al., 2001). Another theory suggests that boys and girls are differentially exposed to certain risk conditions, placing them at variable risk for certain types of delinquency. For example, there is evidence that girls experience a greater number of negative life events during adolescence than boys, and they may, in turn, be more sensitive to their effects, particularly when they emanate from within the home (Ge et al., 1994). Further research is critical to determine the extent to which and how biological factors play a role in differences between girls' delinquent behavior and that of boys.

Stressors, Trauma, and Mental Health

Exposure to severe or cumulative stressors—and responses to them— are strongly associated with risk-taking behavior, including delinquency. Stressors are conditions that elicit strong negative responses and that are perceived as uncontrollable and unpredictable. Such conditions produce alterations in the body's stress responses that disrupt cognitive and emotional

processes, thereby increasing the likelihood of risky behaviors in vulnerable adolescents (McBurnett et al., 2005; Sinha, 2001). Although this is true for both boys and girls, studies have identified some gender differences in rates and types of exposure to stressors. For example, although girls in the juvenile justice system are more likely to have a history of abuse and neglect than nonjustice-involved girls (Berlinger and Elliot, 2002), there is further evidence that girls more often experience certain types of trauma (e.g., sexual abuse and rape) than boys (Hennessey et al., 2004; Snyder, 2000). Many studies of special populations suggest that the incidence of sexual abuse is more pervasive among girls who engage in antisocial behavior, particularly those who engage in violent behavior, than among their male counterparts (Poe-Yamagata and Butts, 1996; Smith, Leve, and Chamberlain, 2006; Snell, 1994). On the other hand, the incidence of physical abuse appears to be more equally distributed between boys and girls in adjudicated populations (Acoca, 1998; Funk, 1999; Henggeler, Edwards, and Borduin, 1987; Lederman et al., 2004; Lenssen et al., 2000; Mason, Zimmerman, and Evans, 1998; Shelton, 2004; Wood et al., 2002), but for both at a much higher rate than in the general population (Leve and Chamberlain, 2004), thus constituting a significant risk factor overall. In addition to gender differences in exposure to certain stressors, girls and boys may also vary in their sensitivity to the same stressor. For example, there is some suggestion

Gender Sensitivity to Risk Factors

Boys and girls experience many of the same risk factors, but they appear to differ in sensitivity to and rates of exposure to these factors. For example, sexual assault is a risk factor for both boys and girls, but the rate of exposure to this risk factor is greater for girls.

that girls may be more sensitive to dysfunction and trauma within the home (Dornfield and Kruttschnitt, 1992; Robertson, Bankier, and Schwartz, 1987; Widom, 1991).

Gender differences have also been noted in mental health risk factors for delinquency. For example, boys outnumber girls by a ratio of 3:1 in the diagnoses of attention-deficit/ hyperactivity disorder (ADHD) and conduct disorder, which are known risk factors for problem behavior and delinquency in boys (Barbaresi et al., 2002; Lahey et al., 1999; Offord, Boyle, and Racine, 1989). Although girls exhibit lower levels of delinquency associated with these disorders (Moffitt et al., 2001; Satterfield and Schell, 1997), mental health problems linked to life stressors and experiences of victimization, such as depression, anxiety, and posttraumatic stress disorder, are diagnosed at much higher rates among girls than boys. Although these disorders are also associated with delinquency among boys, the relationship appears to be much stronger for girls (Teplin et al., 2002).

Early Onset of Puberty

Early puberty in girls has been associated with family dysfunction (Ellis and Garber, 2000; Moffitt et al., 1992). Also, early puberty interacts with mental health disorders, ADHD, and cognitive and emotional deficits to potentially worsen behavioral outcomes (Ge, Conger, and Elder, 1996; Graber et al., 1997; Hayward et al., 1997; Kaltiala-Heino et al., 2003; Orr and Ingersoll, 1995; Rieder and Coupey, 1999). Although the timing of puberty is also a potential risk factor for boys, early maturation creates particular risks for girls because of the development of physical signs of maturity inconsistent with still largely undeveloped cognitive and emotional systems (Graber, Brooks-Gunn, and Warren, 1999).

Several studies suggest that early-maturing girls are more likely to engage in delinquency and other risk-taking behaviors. A longitudinal study of 931 males and females (Graber et al., 2004) found that early onset of puberty among girls continued to predict increased risk behavior into adulthood. Some studies find that compared with other girls, early-maturing girls are at increased threat of various high-risk behaviors such as substance abuse, running away, and truancy (Caspi and

Moffitt, 1991; Flannery, Rowe, and Gulley, 1993; Graber et al., 1997; Kaltiala-Heino et al., 2003, Lanza and Collins, 2002; Paikoff and Brooks-Gunn, 1991; Stattin and Magnusson, 1989; Stice, Presnell, and Bearman, 2001). Early maturation in girls also appears to be a risk factor in exposure to intimate partner violence in adolescence (Foster, Hagan, and Brooks-Gunn, 2004).

Moffitt (1993) contends that adolescents experience a "maturity gap" between their level of biological development and their desire to attain adult status. For some adolescents, delinquency may be an attempt to achieve independence and autonomy from parental control and to evidence maturity in the social realm.

Peer and Parent Relationships and Early Puberty

Early-onset puberty in girls is associated with having an adult boyfriend, which, in turn, affects the association between early puberty and delinquency (Castillo Mezzich et al., 1997). Early-maturing girls are more likely to date at younger ages and to affiliate with older males who may be inclined toward delinquent activity and involve the girls in their antisocial behavior (Stattin and Magnusson, 1990; Weichold, Silbereisen, and Schmitt-Rodermund, 2003).

Among early-maturing girls who undergo a difficult transition to adolescence, the presence of preexisting behavioral problems appears to accentuate vulnerability to delinquency (Ge, Conger, and Elder, 1996). Peer and parent relationships are important factors in explaining links between girls' early maturation and delinquency. The onset of puberty is traditionally associated with increased conflict between parents and teens around issues such as dating, selecting friends, and changing behavioral expectations (Paikoff and Brooks-Gunn, 1991). Using data

on 5,477 females from the National Study of Adolescent Health (Add Health), Haynie (2003) found that earlier puberty among girls was associated with higher levels of delinquency and that conflict with parents, exposure to peer deviance, and involvement in romantic relationships strengthened the link between early puberty and delinquency.

Parents' behaviors also appear to moderate the association between early puberty and later outcomes. Studies have found that early-maturing children whose parents use harsh and inconsistent discipline are more likely to develop behavioral problems than children of parents with more positive parenting styles (Ge et al., 2002).

In this way, harsh parenting amplifies the association between pubertal timing and behavior problems. This result highlights how a biological factor, such as pubertal timing, can interact with parenting processes in predicting behavior problems.

School and Neighborhood Contexts and Early Puberty

Environment has also been shown to play a part in the link between early maturation and vulnerability to delinquency. Findings from Caspi et al. (1993) suggest that the impact of early maturation can be affected by the gender composition of schools. These authors found that early-maturing girls in mixed-gender school settings were at greater risk for delinquency than early-maturing girls in same-gender school settings. Neighborhoods can exert crucial influences as well. In a study of a large and diverse sample from Chicago neighborhoods, Obeidallah et al. (2004) found that girls who experience early-onset puberty and

live in highly disadvantaged neighborhoods—characterized by poverty, high unemployment, and a high percentage of single-parent households—are at significantly greater risk for exhibiting violent behaviors than are those who live in less disadvantaged neighborhoods.

In summary, contextual variables such as school, parenting, and neighborhood may exacerbate or ameliorate the relationships between early puberty and problem outcomes. Early puberty, especially when coupled with family conflict and disadvantaged neighborhoods, is a key gender-sensitive factor in girls' delinquency.

Family Influences

Family issues such as inconsistent or lax supervision and various forms of abuse are some of the most studied links to juvenile delinquency. Researchers theorize that girls have stronger connections to family than boys do throughout life (Gecas and Seff, 1990; Gilligan, 1982; Leonard, 1982) and that this connection often serves as a protective factor. The theory follows that when this protective bond is weakened by instability, violence, sexual abuse, and/or lack of parental supervision, girls may engage in more risk-taking behaviors, which in turn may lead to delinquency.

Parental Supervision and Attachment

Complex family processes such as attachment, parental supervision, and maltreatment are important factors that help explain the difference in the onset of delinquency between girls and boys. In their landmark study, Moffitt and colleagues (2001) followed a cohort of 1,000 male and female children, taking into account extrafamilial factors and individual differences. Eight family factors were significantly correlated with delinquency for both girls and boys.[2] Although most of these factors had a stronger relationship to boys' delinquency than to girls', the difference was relatively small.

Findings on attachment, although commonly more associated with girls than boys, are inconsistent across studies, in part because the concept is difficult to measure.

Findings on effects of parental supervision and monitoring are statistically stronger. Consistent parental supervision and monitoring seem to

protect children and adolescents (girls and boys) from involvement in delinquency (Cernkovich and Giordano, 1987; Hirschi, 1969; Schlossman and Cairns, 1993). In a comprehensive study of family dynamics (Patterson, Crosby, and Vuchinich, 1992), parental monitoring was found to protect youth. Conversely, ineffective parenting practices such as inconsistent discipline and repeated faultfinding frequently followed by explosive outbursts characterized families of delinquent youth more than families of nondelinquent youth. Chamberlain (2003) also documented these types of negative family processes in the backgrounds of delinquent girls.

Family Criminality

Criminality of parents and other family members has long been considered a risk factor for delinquency (Glueck and Glueck, 1950; McCord, 1991; Rowe and Farrington, 1997), but has not been extensively studied in girls. Some qualitative studies in the 1980s suggested that women involved in prostitution and other illegal street-life survival strategies were introduced to this behavior by cousins, young aunts, and other relatives who were themselves heavily involved in street life (e.g., Miller, 1986), and that children of drug-using parents are at high risk for antisocial behavior (Brown and Mills, 1987). Giordano and Mohler-Rockwell (2001) studied the effect of familial criminality on the delinquent involvement of girls in a state juvenile justice facility. Researchers found that family members such as mothers, grandmothers, siblings, and aunts—many of whom were criminally involved—encouraged girls to shoplift and some even taught their daughters to smoke crack.

Similarly, Gaarder and Belknap (2002) studied girls arrested for serious offenses and found that their backgrounds commonly included sexual abuse as

children, victimization by intimate partners, parental deviance, and parental drug use.

Family Instability

Family instability, with consequent disruptions in social ties and continuity of education, also appears to be a factor in the development of erratic or disruptive behavior among youth. Keller and colleagues (2002) focused on parental transitions (i.e., residential moves and/or changes in parental caretakers) among the children of drug-using parents and found that a greater number of transitions were significantly associated with drug use and delinquency by the child. The delinquency effect was the same for boys and girls; the drug use effect was found for girls only. This finding of different effects with regard to gender strengthens support for the argument that girls and boys have different developmental processes which may operate independent of family disruption.

Maltreatment

Empirical evidence consistently suggests that family dysfunction and child maltreatment increase the risk of delinquency and criminal offending in girls (and boys). However, very little is known about how this process works, i.e., the effects of specific types of family risk factors, maltreatment characteristics (victim-perpetrator relationship, the victim's age, the duration of maltreatment), the presence of mediating factors, and gender. Some evidence suggests that the timing and duration of maltreatment, as well as intervening life events, can either strengthen or weaken the negative effects of maltreatment (Ireland, Smith, and Thornberry, 2002; Leiter, Myers, and Zingraff, 1994). Accordingly, it may be premature to conclude that the effect of maltreatment on delinquency development is

greater for girls than for boys or that its effect on girls is greater than that of other risk factors.

Attention to the developmental effects of maltreatment, particularly to effects of childhood physical and sexual abuse, increased dramatically during the 1990s with the publication of findings from several prospective longitudinal studies. These findings indicate that a history of abuse and neglect significantly increases the chances of having both a juvenile and an adult criminal record (Widom, 1989a, 1991). Empirical evidence also indicates that girls who perpetrate violence often have a history of violence committed against them (Herrera and McCloskey, 2001; Margolin and Gordis, 2000; Molnar et al., 2005; Song, Singer, and Anglin, 1998; Spohn, 2000; Widom, 1989a, 1989b, 1989c, 1991, 1995).

In her prospective cohort study, Widom found that children who had experienced severe child abuse or neglect were at significantly higher risk for juvenile arrest compared to the matched control group (Widom and Ames, 1994; Widom and Maxfield, 2001). By young adulthood, those reported as severely abused or neglected as children were 59 percent more likely to have been arrested for any offense as a juvenile and 28 percent more likely to have been arrested for violent crime.

Analyzing family effects on delinquency in a community sample, Herrera and McCloskey (2001) found that girls who had experienced severe child abuse were more than seven times as likely as nonabused girls to commit a violent act that was referred to the juvenile justice system, even when researchers applied statistical controls for co-occurring risk factors in violent families.

Sexual abuse is the most studied type of maltreatment of girls. Existing research focuses primarily on psychological outcomes and has a number of methodological limitations. For example, there is no standardized measure of sexual abuse; researchers often leave it up to respondents to define abuse; prospective studies are rare and often follow subjects for only 12 to 18 months; and control groups are often absent. Nevertheless, among studies that have addressed these concerns, the findings are intriguing. Siegel and Williams (2003) found that, with statistical controls for race and family dysfunction in a study of girls, sexual abuse victims had an increased likelihood of juvenile arrests for violent offenses and adult

arrests for any offense. Widom (1995), however, based on a review of arrest records, found that sexual abuse has no greater impact on criminality than other forms of maltreatment such as severe physical abuse and neglect. (The research did not examine gender differences in these effects.) In Widom's study, the "sexual abuse plus group"— a small sample of boys and girls who had experienced sexual abuse as well as severe neglect or nonsexual physical abuse—were more likely than those in other maltreatment groups and those in the comparison sample to be arrested for running away.

Family Structure

Although early research suggests that youth living in two-parent biological families fare better on a range of developmental outcomes than those in single-parent or alternative structures (Amato and Keith, 1991), this research typically finds that effects of family structure on developmental outcomes such as delinquency are not strong (Hetherington and Kelly, 2002).

More tangible differences in family dynamics or circumstances—such as supervision practices—are largely responsible when study groups have different outcomes. An analysis of data from the National Longitudinal Study of Adolescent Health, using a large national probability sample of adolescents (Manning and Lamb, 2003) found that youth in two-parent biological families had more favorable adolescent outcomes than youth with other family structures, including lower levels of reported delinquency involvement. Youth living in families in which the mother was cohabiting with an unmarried partner had worse outcomes than those in stepparent families. A gender-specific analysis of the Add Health data (Demuth and Brown, 2004) found that a mother's cohabitation had similar effects on the likelihood of involvement in delinquency for both boys and girls. The highest rates of delinquency were for youth in father-only households, followed by father–stepmother and single-mother households.

The Impact of Peers

Research has consistently documented the importance of friendship and peers in adolescent behavior and delinquency (Warr, 2002). Empirical studies suggest that unstructured socializing among youth—socializing without specific activities and without guidance or supervision by positive adults—increases the likelihood that delinquent activities will occur (Coie, Dodge, and Kupersmidt, 1990; Mahoney and Stattin, 2000). Studies further document that boys and girls who engage in highly structured activities associated with school and prosocial clubs are less likely to become involved in delinquent behavior than peers without this involvement (Eccles and Barber, 1999; Mahoney and Cairns, 1997; Mahoney, Cairns, and Farmer, 2003; Mahoney and Stattin, 2000).

Family Structure and Delinquency

The likelihood of delinquency effects of family structure were statistically weak and indirect and were further weakened when family processes such as parental supervision and maltreatment were taken into account (Demuth and Brown, 2004).

Empirical studies also have examined the effect of social skill deficits—i.e., whether young people who are unsuccessful with peers are more likely to become antisocial and aggressive. Moffitt and colleagues (2001) found that boys and girls who were rejected by other children during the grade school years were more likely to become delinquent; this effect was stronger for boys. Conversely, Cairns and Cairns (1994) found that aggressive boys and girls were generally solid members of peer clusters rather than socially isolated and had as many friendships as nonaggressive youth.

Adolescents' social connections may also provide support for and training in delinquent behavior (Morash, 1986; Jensen, 2003), amplify risk-taking, and foster and reinforce a delinquent view of self (Matsueda, 1992). Aggressive youth often affiliate with other aggressive youth (Cairns and Cairns, 1994). This social context provides an opportunity for modeling aggressive behavior and a buffer against the social disapproval of others. Peer influence of this sort is a critical factor in understanding adolescent involvement in delinquency. A study of high-school-age girls found that those who had been adjudicated as delinquent offenders reported greater levels of perceived peer pressure than other girls (Claes and Simard, 1992; Giordano, Cernkovich, and Pugh, 1986).

In an analysis of Add Health data, Haynie (2001) found that peers' delinquency had a significant effect on a youth's own delinquency, as did the cohesiveness of the peer network. The majority of adolescents in this nationally representative sample reported a mix of friendships, including delinquent and nondelinquent friends. However, youth involved with the highest level of delinquency reported that almost all their friends were delinquent (Haynie, 2002). The focus of this research was

not on gender differences, so no analyses by gender were conducted, however, the findings suggest important dynamics for further research.

Delinquency happens most often in group contexts. As noted earlier, girls' association with males is a factor in the onset and course of delinquency. Stattin and Magnusson (1990) suggest that girls' early maturation may influence their association with older males and, in turn, increase their risk for delinquent behavior if the older male is involved in delinquent activities. Analyses of Add Health data found that romantic partners' delinquency did influence respondents' likelihood of delinquency (Haynie et al., 2005)—a dynamic that has stronger relevance for girls' delinquency than for boys'.

Girls may adopt drug and alcohol use to cope with partner abuse, to win their partner's approval, or to fit in with peers (Giordano, Cernkovich, and Rossol, 2002). Violence related to jealousy and other relationship problems may also contribute to girls' delinquency (Miller and White, 2003).

Neighborhood Effects

The research literature on how neighborhoods affect residents' behavior is extensive, and a growing number of studies are examining how exposure to violence in neighborhoods or schools affects youth (Margolin and Gordis, 2000). (See Kroneman, Loeber, and Hipwell, 2004, for a review of neighborhood context, delinquency, and gender.)

The literature on the effects of neighborhoods reflects a long history of sociological and public health research, focusing primarily on social disorganization (Sampson, Morenoff, and Gannon-Rowley, 2002; Bursik and

Grasmick, 1993a,b), as well as research by developmental psychologists (Brooks-Gunn et al., 1993, 2000; Jencks and Mayer, 1990) and economists (Durlauf, 2004). Literature reviews have been conducted in each of these areas (Sampson, Morenoff, and Gannon-Rowley, 2002; Leventhal and Brooks-Gunn, 2000; Durlauf, 2004).

Neighborhood characteristics examined in these studies include concentrated poverty, household structure, social cohesion or disorganization, social capital and efficacy, and residential mobility. These studies explored how these neighborhood characteristics relate to risky behaviors, early school attrition, health outcomes, exposure to and use of violence, and crime and delinquency.

In general, researchers have found that neighborhoods with structural disadvantage or concentrated poverty have higher rates of violence (Messner, Raffalovich, and McMillan, 2001; Lauritsen and White, 2001), violent victimization and exposure to violence (Farrell and Bruce, 1997; Molnar et al., 2005), and arrests for property and personal crime (Steffensmeier and Haynie, 2000). The impact of neighborhood characteristics on girls versus boys has not been extensively researched. Some studies suggest that girls are, in general, more closely supervised and kept closer to the home than are boys; thus, girls are less exposed than boys to the street violence found in many disadvantaged neighborhoods (Farrell and Bruce, 1997; Bottcher, 2001). The finding that girls are also less likely than boys to be expelled from school for misconduct (Clark et al., 2003) suggests that they are less exposed to neighborhood environments. Although girls are less often exposed to violence in the community than boys are, girls who are exposed to violence exhibit more violence than nonvictimized girls in similar neighborhoods (Molnar et al., 2005).

Violent Behavior

Research has shown interactions between neighborhood characteristics, prior violent victimization, and violent behavior. For example, findings from a prospective study of violence by girls based on a large and diverse sample from Chicago neighborhoods found that adolescent girls were more likely to act violently if they had been victims of violence and if they lived in communities with high rates of poverty and/or violent crime. Even when researchers took into consideration socioeconomic status, previous perpetration of violence, deviant peer behavior, illegal substance use, and other family and individual characteristics, violent victimization remained an important risk factor for subsequent violent behavior by girls. Girls between ages 9 and 15 were 2.4 times as likely to engage in violence if they had a history of prior physical or sexual molestation/ assault or had been otherwise violently victimized at home, at school, or in the community. Girls living in economically disadvantaged neighborhoods were 1.5 times as likely to behave violently as girls in other neighborhoods. Victimized girls in violent, economically disadvantaged neighborhoods were twice as likely to behave violently as nonvictimized girls in similar neighborhoods (Molnar et al., 2005).

The impacts of neighborhood disadvantage on violent outcomes are echoed in other studies. In a survey of African American youth, Farrell and Bruce (1997) found that higher levels of exposure to violence in disadvantaged neighborhoods led to increased

Positive Effects of Relocation

Relocation to more affluent neighborhoods lowered the rate of girls' arrests for violent and property offenses.

violent behavior by both girls and boys. Lauritsen and White (2001) also found that nonstranger violence was higher for both black and white females when they lived in disadvantaged neighborhoods.

Lane, Cunningham, and Ellen (2004) studied knife and gun carrying—typically measures of more violent behavior— among a sample of low-income African American girls and boys in San Francisco. Boys and girls did not differ in their intent to carry knives, and this intent was associated with more delinquent and aggressive behaviors in both genders. Boys, as other studies have found, were more likely than girls to carry guns.

Relocation

One study has examined the effects of moving away from disadvantaged neighborhoods on later delinquency. In the Moving to Opportunity study (Kling, Ludwig, and Katz, 2005), public housing residents in five cities were randomly assigned to an experimental group in which residents could use a housing voucher to relocate to a leased unit in a nonpoverty area. A control group received no vouchers. Researchers used arrest data and survey information to analyze delinquency among boys and girls in the two groups.

Both girls and boys in the experimental group (the group receiving vouchers) experienced fewer arrests for violent offenses compared with youth in the control group that did not relocate. Girls in the experimental group were also arrested less often for other crimes. However, several years after the move occurred, the effects changed for males. Property crime arrests became more common for boys who had moved to more affluent neighborhoods than for boys who had not moved, although violent crime by the boys who moved

remained low. Arrests for both violent and property crime remained low for girls who moved. The move to a better neighborhood also appeared to improve girls' expectations for completing college, increased their participation in sports, and was associated with reduced school absences and increased associations with peers who engaged in school activities.

Differential Effects of Disadvantaged Neighborhoods

Current studies suggest that disadvantaged neighborhoods are somewhat less of a risk factor for delinquency in girls than in boys because girls are more closely supervised and kept closer to home. Nevertheless, neighborhoods remain important influences on girls' involvement in both violence and less serious forms of delinquency. Additional research is needed to examine the nature and extent of that influence more closely.

Involvement in Religious Activities

The construct of religiosity, in particular, is difficult to measure. Surveys have used varied approaches to measuring religiosity (e.g., single-item measure versus multiple-item measure) and this has led to inconsistent findings in research (Johnson et al., 2000).

Some studies suggest that religion plays a role in regulating antisocial behavior among youth. Involvement in religion-focused activities may affect socialization and behaviors, especially among very cohesive religious groups. However, these studies tend to be small, use limited measurements, and lack controls for external variables (Johnson, 2002; Smith, 2005).

Many youth report some involvement in religion. A recent article summarizing multiple surveys on teens' religious behavior found that the majority of teens claim some sort of religious affiliation (Smith et al., 2003).

Studies suggest that involvement in religious activities can protect against minor delinquency (Baier and Wright, 2001). Consistent with findings about peer and other social affiliations, this effect is more likely when teens are surrounded by others involved with religion, including parents, peers, and community residents (Pearce and Haynie, 2004; Regnerus, 2003; Stark, Kent, and Doyle, 1982). Parents' religiosity also seems to have protective effects on delinquency among youth, although this appears stronger for boys than girls (Regnerus and Elder, 2003). Studies further suggest that having religious parents effectively discourages delinquency only when the child is also religious (Pearce and Haynie, 2004).

Various theories have been used to explain why involvement in religion may protect against delinquency. For instance, strain theory argues that religion may reduce the stressors that adolescents face (Agnew, 2001). Some studies report that religious adolescents are more likely to get along well with their parents or other adults, feel more comfortable talking with adults, have more adults they can turn to for support, and are less likely to associate with delinquent peers (Jang and Johnson, 2005; Regnerus, 2003; Sherkat and Ellison, 1999; Smith, 2005). Control theory suggests that religious teens may be more under their parents' control, have higher stakes in conformity to mainstream social norms, and may be more invested in maintaining a positive image (Jang and Johnson, 2001; Johnson et al., 2001; Regnerus, 2003; Regnerus and Elder, 2003; Sherkat and Ellison, 1999; Smith, 2005).

Schools

Academic Performance

Much research has been conducted on the general relationship between academic performance and deviant behavior (Gottfredson, 1981, 2001; Junger-Tas, Ribeaud, and Cruyff, 2004; Maguin and Loeber, 1996; Paulson, Coombs, and Richardson, 1990; Rosay et al., 2000). The inverse relationship between academic performance and deviance seems stronger in boys than in girls (Junger-Tas, Ribeaud, and Cruyff, 2004; Maguin and Loeber, 1996). However, gender differences appear to depend on the type of deviant behavior studied.

Some studies have found that the inverse relationship between academic performance and drug use is equal for both genders (Paulson, Coombs and Richardson, 1990; Rosay et al., 2000).

Attachment to School

Attachment to school generally is defined as the extent to which students care about school and about teachers' opinion of them. The more students feel as though they belong to their school, the less likely they are to engage in delinquent behavior (Cernkovich and Giordano, 1992; Gottfredson, Wilson, and Najaka, 2002; Jenkins, 1997; Liska and Reed, 1985; Welsh, Greene, and Jenkins, 1999). This relationship is well documented in both cross-sectional and longitudinal studies; although some studies found a protective effect for girls only (Crosnoe, Erickson, and Dornbusch, 2002; Sale et al., 2003), most studies demonstrate that the protective effect of attachment is equal for boys and girls (Cernkovich and Giordano, 1992; Zweig et al., 2002). An analysis of the Add Health data for 12,578 adolescent students found that boys and girls with low-risk profiles reported more school connectedness than those with higher risk profiles (Zweig et al., 2002).

Longitudinal studies, which provide a more solid base for examining gender differences in the relationship between school attachment and delinquency, indicate that attachment has a stronger influence for girls than boys: Crosnoe, Erickson, and Dornbusch (2002) found that bonding with teachers protected against delinquency, even when girls had delinquent friends.

Commitment to School

Commitment to school is generally defined as the time and energy invested by students in the pursuit of their educational goals. Students who spend a considerable amount of time and effort in school are more likely to be concerned about losing their investment if they engage in deviant behavior, whereas students who have little invested and less to lose are more likely to engage in deviant behavior. As with findings on attachment to school, this relationship is well documented in both cross-sectional and longitudinal studies (Cernkovich and Giordano, 1992; Gottfredson, 2001; Gottfredson, Wilson, and Najaka, 2002; Jenkins, 1997; Thornberry, Esbensen, and Van Kammen, 1993; Thornberry et al., 1991; Welsh, Greene, and Jenkins, 1999).

School-Level Factors

The research suggests that most school-level factors affect girls and boys equally when it comes to delinquency. School-level factors include grade level, size of student enrollment, class size, racial and ethnic composition, and school location. A key factor in the development of delinquency in youth is students' perception of whether rules are clear and enforced fairly and the impact of unusual or punitive responses to misbehavior (Payne and Gottfredson, 2005). Perception of fairness protects against delinquent behavior for both genders, but more so for boys than for girls.

Empirical literature to date indicates that attachment to school has protective effects against delinquency for both genders, although several recent studies find a stronger effect for girls. Academic performance, clarity of rules, and a perception of the rules and their enforcement as fair also are protective for both genders but seem to have a stronger effect for boys.

Justice System Responses to Girls

Historically, juvenile courts primarily dealt with boys under delinquency jurisdiction and girls under status offense jurisdiction (Feld, 2009b). This distinction has often led to different processing of female status offenders in courts and in mental health and juvenile justice institutions. The Juvenile Justice and Delinquency Prevention Act of 1974 provided impetus to divert, deinstitutionalize, and decriminalize all status offenders. Although the Act restricted commitment of status offenders to training schools, states did not provide adequate community-based alternatives for girls (American Bar Association and National Bar Association, 2001). Female status offenders were relabeled as "delinquent" and often confined in private-sector mental health and chemical dependency treatment facilities, or were placed in detention as a protective strategy when other placements were not available (Snyder and Sickmund, 2006; Weithorn, 1988).

As noted earlier, girls accounted for about a quarter (23 percent) of all juveniles arrested for aggravated assault in 2006 and about a third (34 percent) of those arrested for other assaults. Between 1980 to 2006, while boys' arrest rate for simple assault doubled, the arrest rate for simple assault for girls quadrupled. Percentage increases in assault arrest rates for girls reflect, in part, girls' relatively low rates of assault offenses compared to boys' (Chesney-Lind and Shelden, 1998; Steffensmeier et al., 2005). The literature suggests no major increase in violent behavior among adolescent girls, despite a major increase in their arrests for simple assault (Steffensmeier et al., 2005). The changes in numbers, rates, and gender ratios for assault offenses suggest a relabeling of status offenses (e.g., incorrigibility) as domestic violence assaults. When police implemented policies of zero tolerance and mandatory arrests for domestic assailants in the 1990s, events previously recorded as family disputes may have come to be reclassified as simple or aggravated assault. Police also may have begun to treat threats to do harm much more seriously.

Implications for Program and Policy Development

The results of this literature review suggest that risk and protective factors for girls' delinquency are, in many ways, similar to risk and protective factors for boys' delinquency. However, key gender differences exist, with important implications for program and policy development.

Important areas for consideration in programming and policy include:

- Delinquency prevention and intervention programs for girls must address physical maltreatment,

including sexual abuse and assault. Compared to boys, girls experience more sexual abuse in the home and are at greater risk for sexual assault outside the home (Berlinger and Elliot, 2002).

■ Responses to mental health problems such as depression, anxiety, and posttraumatic stress disorder should be integral components of programming for girls. Depression and anxiety are more frequently diagnosed in girls than in boys and may accompany delinquency. Aggression by girls may indicate earlier victimization and signify that these girls need intervention to deal with these experiences. An increase in family-centered programming may be useful.

■ Lack of family supervision and monitoring has a causal link to delinquency for both boys and girls. Ineffective parenting practices, including harsh or inconsistent discipline, are critical factors in the development of girls' delinquency. Parental deviance, family criminality, and parental drug use are strongly associated with the development of delinquent and criminal behavior in children and adolescents of both genders.

■ Positive school involvement protects against delinquency in both girls and boys. School attachment is more significant for girls than for boys, while rule fairness and enforcement are more significant for boys.

■ As evidenced by the results of the Moving to Opportunity Study, attention to neighborhood effects and programs that facilitate moves to affluent neighborhoods may be especially helpful to girls.

■ Interdisciplinary models that place behaviors in social, psychological, and biological context for girls

are critical in understanding and responding to early puberty as a risk factor. Helping girls who enter puberty early to understand and deal with peer and parental response is one way of offsetting some of the biological/emotional maturity disconnect.

■ The link between girls' delinquent behavior and system responses remains an important area for policy, programs, and research. The American Bar Association and National Bar Association report *Justice by Gender* (2001) notes a critical lack of prevention, diversion, and treatment alternatives for girls in the juvenile justice system.

Conclusion

Although additional research is critically needed, it is clear that factors such as economic disadvantage, exposure to violence, experiences with physical and sexual child abuse and maltreatment, and lack of positive parental supervision affect the development of delinquency for both girls and boys. Early puberty, coupled with stressors such as conflict with parents and involvement with delinquent (and often older) male peers, is a risk factor unique to girls.

These factors must be addressed in efforts to understand and address girls' delinquency. Finally, two aspects of the justice system also merit examination: arrest policies that widen the net (especially those dealing with conflicts between adolescent girls and their parents) and detention of girls because community-based alternatives are lacking. See Feld (2009a) for additional discussion.

Endnotes

1. Survival sex is offered for food, shelter, protection, or money; prostitution is engaged in strictly for money.

2. The eight factors that were significantly correlated with girls' delinquency were as follows: (1) negative and critical mothers, (2) harsh discipline, (3) inconsistent discipline, (4) family conflict, (5) frequent family moves, (6) multiple caregivers, (7) longer periods of time with a single parent, and (8) growing up in socioeconomically disadvantaged families.

References

Acoca, L. 1998. Outside/inside: The violation of American girls at home, on the streets, and in the juvenile justice system. *Crime and Delinquency* 44:561–589.

Agnew, R. 2001. Building on the foundation of General Strain Theory: Specifying the types of strain most likely to lead to crime and delinquency. *Journal of Research in Crime and Delinquency* 38:319–361.

Amato, P.R., and Keith, B. 1991. Parental divorce and the well-being of children: A meta-analysis. *Psychological Bulletin* 110:26–46.

American Bar Association and National Bar Association. 2001. *Justice by Gender: The Lack of Appropriate Prevention, Diversion, and Treatment Alternatives for Girls in the Justice System.* Washington, DC: American Bar Association and National Bar Association.

Baier, C.J., and Wright, B.R.E. 2001. "If you love me, keep my commandments": A meta-analysis of the effect of religion on crime. *Journal of Research in Crime and Delinquency* 38:3–21.

Barbaresi, W.J., Katusic, S.K., Colligan, R.C., Pankratz, V.S., Weaver, A.L., Weber, K.J., Mrazek, D.A., and Jacobsen, S.J. 2002. How common is attention-deficit/hyperactivity disorder?: Incidence in a population-based birth cohort in Rochester, Minnesota. *Archives of Pediatrics and Adolescent Medicine* 156:217–224.

Berlinger, L., and Elliot, D.M. 2002. Sexual abuse of children. In *The APSAC Handbook on Child Maltreatment. Second Edition.* Thousand Oaks, CA: Sage Publications, Inc., pp. 55–78.

Bottcher, J. 2001. Social practices of gender: How gender relates to delinquency in the everyday lives of high-risk youths. *Criminology* 39(4):893–932.

Brooks-Gunn, J., Duncan, G.J., Klebanov, P.K., and Sealand, N. 1993. Do neighborhoods influence child and adolescent development? *American Journal of Sociology* 99(2):353–395.

Brooks-Gunn, J., Duncan, G.J., Leventhal, T., and Aber, J.L. 2000. Lessons learned and future directions for research on the neighborhoods in which children live. In *Neighborhood Poverty, Vol. 1: Context and Consequences for Children,* edited by J. Brooks-Gunn, G.J. Duncan, and J.L. Aber. New York, NY: Russell Sage Foundation, pp. 279–298.

Brown, B.S., and Mills, A.R., eds. 1987. *Youth at High Risk for Substance Abuse.* Rockville, MD: U.S. Department of Health and Human Services, National Institute on Drug Abuse.

Brown, L.M. 1998. *Raising Their Voices: The Politics of Girls' Anger.* Cambridge, MA: Harvard University Press.

Bursik, R.J., and Grasmick, H.G. 1993a. The criminal behavior of neighborhood residents. In *Neighborhoods and Crime: The Dimensions of Effective Community Control.* New York, NY: Lexington Books, pp. 24–59.

Bursik, R.J., and Grasmick, H.G. 1993b. Neighborhood opportunities for criminal behavior. In *Neighborhoods and Crime: The Dimensions of Effective Community Control.* New York, NY: Lexington Books, pp. 60–89.

Cairns, R.B., and Cairns, B.D. 1994. *Lifelines and Risks: Pathways of Youth in Our Time.* New York, NY: Cambridge University Press.

Caspi, A., and Moffitt, T.E. 1991. Individual differences are accentuated during periods of social change: The sample case of girls at puberty. *Journal of Personality and Social Psychology* 61:157–168.

Caspi, A., Lynam, D.R., Moffitt, T.E., and Silva, P.A. 1993. Unraveling girls' delinquency: Biological, dispositional, and contextual contributions to adolescent misbehavior. *Developmental Psychology* 29:19–30.

Castillo Mezzich, A., Tarter, R.E., Giancola, P.R., Lu, S., Kirisci, L., and Parks, S. 1997. Substance use and risky sexual behavior in female adolescents. *Drug and Alcohol Dependence* 44(2–3):157–166.

Cernkovich, S.A., and Giordano, P.C. 1987. Family relationships and delinquency. *Criminology* 25:295–321.

Cernkovich, S.A., and Giordano, P.C. 1992. School bonding, race, and delinquency. *Criminology* 30:261–287.

Chamberlain, P. 2003. *Treating Chronic Juvenile Offenders: Advances Made Through the Oregon Multidimensional Treatment Foster Care Model.* Washington, DC: American Psychological Association.

Champion, H.L.O., and Durant, R.H. 2001. Exposure to violence and victimization and the use of violence by adolescents in the United States. *Minerva Pediatrica* 53:189–197.

Chesney-Lind, M., and Shelden, R.G. 1998. *Girls, Delinquency, and Juvenile Justice.* Belmont, WA: Wadsworth.

Claes, M., and Simard R. 1992. Friendship characteristics of delinquent adolescents. *International Journal of Adolescence and Youth* 3:287–301.

Clark, M.D., Petras, H., Kellam, S.G., Ialongo, N., and Poduska, J.M. 2003. Who's most at risk for school removal and later juvenile delinquency? Effects of early risk factors, gender, school/community poverty, and their impact on more distal outcomes. *Women and Criminal Justice* 14:89–116.

Coie, J.D., Dodge, K.A., and Kupersmidt, J.B. 1990. Peer group behavior and social status. In *Peer Rejection in Childhood,* edited by S. Asher and J.D. Coie. New York, NY: Cambridge University Press, pp. 17–59.

Crosnoe, R., Erickson, K.G., and Dornbusch, S.M. 2002. Protective functions of family relationships and school factors on the deviant behavior of adolescent boys and girls. *Youth and Society* 33(4):515–544.

Demuth, S., and Brown, S.L. 2004. Family structure, family processes, and adolescent delinquency: The significance of parental absence versus parental gender. *Journal of Research in Crime and Delinquency* 41:58–81.

Dornfield, M., and Kruttschnitt, C. 1992. Do the stereotypes fit? Mapping gender-specific outcomes and risk factors. *Criminology* 30(3):397–419.

Durlauf, S.N. 2004. Neighborhood effects. In *Handbook of Regional and Urban Economics, Vol. 4, Cities and Geography,* Part I: Cities and urban systems: From theory to facts, edited by J.V. Henderson and J.F. Thisse. New York, NY: North-Holland/Elsevier, pp. 2173–2242.

Eccles, J.S., and Barber, B.L. 1999. Student council, volunteering, basketball, or marching band: What kind of extracurricular involvement matters? *Journal of Adolescent Research* 14:10–43.

Ellis, B.J., and Garber, J. 2000. Psychosocial antecedents of variation in girls' pubertal timing: Maternal depression, stepfather presence, and marital and family stress. *Child Development* 71:485–501.

Farrell, A.D., and Bruce, S.E. 1997. Impact of exposure to community violence on violent behavior and emotional distress among urban adolescents. *Journal of Clinical Child Psychology* 26(1):2–14.

Feitel, B., Margetson, N., Chamas, J., and Lipman, C. 1992. Psychosocial background and behavioral and emotional disorders of homeless and runaway youth. *Hospital and Community Psychiatry* 43:155–159.

Feld, B. 2009a. Girls in the juvenile justice system. In *The Delinquent Girl,* edited by Margaret A. Zahn. Philadelphia, PA: Temple University Press, pp. 225–264.

Feld, B. 2009b. Violent girls or relabeled offender? An alternative interpretation of the data. *Crime and Delinquency* 55(2): 241–265 [Special Issue: Gender Issues in Juvenile and Criminal Justice].

Flannery, D.J., Rowe, D.C., and Gulley, B.L. 1993. Impact of pubertal status, timing, and age on adolescent sexual experience and delinquency. *Journal of Adolescent Research* 8:21–40.

Foster, H., Hagan, J., and Brooks-Gunn, J. 2004. Age, puberty, and exposure to intimate partner violence in adolescence. *Annals of the New York Academy of Sciences* 1036: 151–166.

Funk, S.J. 1999. Risk assessment for juveniles on probation: A focus on gender. *Criminal Justice and Behavior* 26:44–68.

Gaarder, E., and Belknap, J. 2002. Tenuous borders: Girls transferred to adult court. *Criminology* 40:481–517.

Ge, X., Brody, G.H., Conger, R.D., Simons, R.L., and Murry, V.M. 2002. Contextual amplification of the effects of pubertal transition on African-American children's deviant peer affiliation and externalized behavioral problems. *Developmental Psychology* 38:42–54.

Ge, X., Conger, R.D., and Elder, G.H. 1996. Coming of age too early: Pubertal influences on girls' vulnerability to psychological distress. *Child Development* 67:3386–3400.

Ge, X., Conger, R.D., Lorenz, F.O., and Simons, R.L. 1994. Parents' stressful life events and adolescent depressed mood. *Journal of Health and Social Behavior* 35:28–44.

Gecas, V., and Seff, M. 1990. Social class and self-esteem: Psychological centrality, compensation, and the relative effects of work and home. *Social Psychology Quarterly* 53(2):165–173.

Gilligan, C. 1982. *In a Different Voice: Psychological Theory and Women's Development.* Cambridge, MA: Harvard University Press.

Giordano, P.C., Cernkovich, S.A., and Pugh, M.D. 1986. Friendships and delinquency. *American Journal of Sociology* 91:1170–1202.

Giordano, P.C., Cernkovich, S.A., and Rossol, J. 2002. Emotion, cognition, and crime. Paper presented at the annual meeting of the American Sociological Association, Chicago, IL.

Giordano, P.C., and Mohler-Rockwell, S. 2001. Differential association theory and female crime. In *Of Crime and Criminality: The Use of Theory in Everyday Life,* edited by S. Simpson. Thousand Oaks, CA: Pine Forge Press.

Glueck, S., and Glueck, E. 1950. *Unraveling Juvenile Delinquency.* Cambridge, MA: Harvard University Press.

Gottfredson, D.C. 2001. *Delinquency and Schools.* New York, NY: Cambridge University Press.

Gottfredson, D.C., Wilson, D.B., and Najaka, S.S. 2002. School-based crime prevention. In *Evidence-Based Crime Prevention,* edited by L.W. Sherman, D.P. Farrington, B.C. Welsh, and D.L. MacKenzie. London, England: Routledge.

Gottfredson, G.D. 1981. Schooling and delinquency. In *New Directions in the Rehabilitation of Criminal Offenders,* edited by S.E. Martin, L.B. Sechrest, and R. Redner. Washington, DC: National Academy Press, pp. 424–469.

Graber, J.A., Brooks-Gunn, J., and Warren, M.P. 1999. The vulnerable transition: Puberty and the development of eating pathology and negative mood. *Women's Health Issues* 9:107–114.

Graber, J.A., Lewinsohn, P.M., Seeley, J.R., and Brooks-Gunn, J. 1997. Is psychopathology associated with the timing of pubertal development? *Journal of the American Academy of Child and Adolescent Psychiatry* 36(12):1768–1776.

Graber, J.A., Seeley, J.R., Brooks-Gunn, J., and Lewinsohn, P.M. 2004. Is pubertal timing associated with psychopathology in young adulthood? *Journal of the American Academy of Child and Adolescent Psychiatry* 43(6):718–726.

Haynie, D.L. 2001. Delinquent peers revisited: Does network structure matter? *American Journal of Sociology* 106:1013–1057.

Haynie, D.L. 2002. Friendship networks and delinquency: The relative nature of peer delinquency. *Journal of Quantitative Criminology* 18(2):99–134.

Haynie, D.L. 2003. Contexts of risk? Explaining the link between girls' pubertal development and their delinquency involvement. *Social Forces* 82:355–397.

Haynie, D.L., Giordano, P.C., Manning, W., and Longmore, M.A. 2005. Adolescent romantic relationships and delinquency involvement. *Criminology* 43(1):177–210.

Hayward, C., Killen, J.D., Wilson, D.M., Hammer, L.D., Litt, I.F., Kraemer, H.C., Haydel, F., Varady, A., and Taylor, C.B. 1997. Psychiatric risk associated with early puberty in adolescent girls. *Journal of the American Academy of Child and Adolescent Psychiatry* 36(2):255–262.

Henggeler, S.W., Edwards, J., and Borduin, C.M. 1987. The family relations of female juvenile delinquents. *Journal of Abnormal Child Psychology* 15:199–209.

Hennessey, M., Ford, J.D., Mahoney, K., Ko, S.J., and Siegfried, C.B. 2004. *Trauma Among Girls in the Juvenile Justice System.* Los Angeles, CA: National Child Traumatic Stress Network.

Herrera, V.M., and McCloskey, L.A. 2001. Gender differences in the risk for delinquency among youth exposed to family violence. *Child Abuse and Neglect* 25:1037–1052.

Hetherington, E.M., and Kelly, J. 2002. *For Better or for Worse: Divorce Reconsidered.* New York, NY: W.W. Norton and Company.

Hirschi, T. 1969. *Causes of Delinquency.* Berkeley, CA: University of California Press.

Ireland, T.O., Smith, C.A., and Thornberry, T.P. 2002. Developmental issues in the impact of child maltreatment on later delinquency and drug use. *Criminology* 40:359–399.

Jang, S.J., and Johnson, B.R. 2001. Neighborhood disorder, individual religiosity, and adolescent use of illicit drugs: A test of multilevel hypotheses. *Criminology* 39:109–144.

Jang, S.J., and Johnson, B.R. 2005. Gender, religiosity, and reactions to strain among African Americans. *Sociological Quarterly* 46:323–357.

Jencks, C., and Mayer, S.E. 1990. The social consequences of growing up in a poor neighborhood. In *Inner-City Poverty in the United States,* edited by L.E. Lynn and M.G.H. McGeary. Washington, DC: National Academies Press, pp. 111–186.

Jenkins, P.H. 1997. School delinquency and the school social bond. *Journal of Research in Crime and Delinquency* 34(3):337–368.

Jensen, G.F. 2003. Gender variation in delinquency: Self-images, beliefs, and peers as mediating mechanisms. In *Social Learning Theory and the Explanations of Crime,* edited by R.L. Akers and G.F. Jensen. New Brunswick, NJ: Transaction.

Johnson, B.M. 2002. Friendships among delinquent adolescent girls: Why do some select males as their closest friends? Unpublished doctoral dissertation, University of California, Los Angeles.

Johnson, B.R., De Li, S., Larson, D.B., and McCullough, M. 2000. A systematic review of the religiosity and delinquency literature: A research note. *Journal of Contemporary Criminal Justice* 16:32–52.

Johnson, B.R., Jang, S.J., Larson, D.B., and De Li, S. 2001. Does adolescent religious commitment matter? A reexamination of the effects of religiosity on delinquency. *Journal of Research in Crime and Delinquency* 38:22–44.

Junger-Tas, J., Ribeaud, D., and Cruyff, M.J.L.F. 2004. Juvenile delinquency and gender. *European Journal of Criminology* 1(3):333–375.

Kaltiala-Heino, R., Marttunen, M., Rantanen, P., and Rimpela, M. 2003. Early puberty is associated with mental health problems in middle adolescence. *Social Science and Medicine* 57:1055–1064.

Keller, T.E., Catalano. R.F., Haggerty, K.P., and Fleming, C.B. 2002. Parent figure transitions and delinquency and drug use among early adolescent children of substance abusers. *The American Journal of Drug and Alcohol Abuse* 28:399–427.

Klein, L.C., and Corwin, E.J. 2002. Seeing the unexpected: How sex differences in stress responses may provide a new perspective on the manifestation of psychiatric disorders. *Current Psychiatry Reports* 4(6):441–448.

Kling, J.R., Ludwig, J., and Katz, L.F. 2005. Neighborhood effects on crime for female and male youth: Evidence from a randomized housing voucher experiment. *Quarterly Journal of Economics* 120:87–130.

Kroneman, L., Loeber, R., and Hipwell, A.E. 2004. Is neighborhood context differently related to externalizing problems and delinquency for girls compared with boys? *Clinical Child and Family Psychology Review* 7(2):109–122.

Lahey, B.B., Goodman, S.H., Waldman, I.D., Bird, H., Canino, G., Jensen, P., Regier, D., Leaf, P.J., Gordon, R., and Applegate, B. 1999. Relation of age of onset to the type and severity of child and adolescent conduct problems. *Journal of Abnormal Child Psychology* 27:247–260.

Lane, M.A., Cunningham, S.D., and Ellen, J.M. 2004. The intention of adolescents to carry a knife or a gun: A study of low-income African-American adolescents. *Journal of Adolescent Health* 34(1):72–78.

Lanza, S.T., and Collins, L.M. 2002. Pubertal timing and the onset of substance use in females during early adolescence. *Prevention Science* 3:69–82.

Lauritsen, J.L., and White, N.A. 2001. Putting violence in its place: The influence of race, ethnicity, gender, and place on the risk for violence. *Criminology and Public Policy* 1(1):37–59.

Lederman, C.S., Dakof, G.A., Larrea, M.A., and Li, H. 2004. Characteristics of adolescent females in juvenile detention. *International Journal of Law and Psychiatry* 27:321–337.

Leiter, J., Myers, K.A., and Zingraff, M.T. 1994. Substantiated and unsubstantiated cases of child maltreatment: Do their consequences differ? *Social Work Research* 18:67–82.

Leitz, L. 2003. Girl fights: Exploring females' resistance to educational structures. *International Journal of Sociology and Social Policy* 23(11):15–43.

Lenssen, S.A., Doreleijers, T.A., Van Dijk, M.E., and Hartman, C.A. 2000. Girls in detention: What are their characteristics? A project to explore and document the character of this target group and the significant ways in which it differs from one consisting of boys. *Journal of Adolescence* 23:287–303.

Leonard, E.B. 1982. *Women, Crime and Society: A Critique of Theoretical Criminology.* New York, NY: Longman.

Leve, L.D., and Chamberlain, P. 2004. Female juvenile offenders: Defining an early-onset pathway for delinquency. *Journal of Child and Family Studies* 13(4):439–452.

Leventhal, T., and Brooks-Gunn., J. 2000. The neighborhoods they live in: The effects of neighborhood residence on child and adolescent outcomes. *Psychological Bulletin* 126(2):309–337.

Liska, A., and Reed, M. 1985. Ties to conventional institutions and delinquency: Estimating reciprocal effects. *American Sociological Review* 50:547–560.

Lockwood, D. 1997. *Violence Among Middle School and High School Students: Analyses and Implications for Prevention.* Research in Brief. Washington, DC: U.S. Department of Justice, Office of Justice Programs, National Institute of Justice.

Maguin, E., and Loeber, R. 1996. Academic performance and delinquency. In *Crime and Justice: A Review of Research,* vol. 20, edited by M. Tonry. Chicago, IL: University of Chicago Press.

Mahoney, J.L., and Cairns, R.B. 1997. Do extracurricular activities protect against early school dropout? *Developmental Psychology* 32:241–253.

Mahoney, J.L., Cairns, B.D., and Farmer, T.W. 2003. Promoting interpersonal competence and educational success through extracurricular activity participation. *Journal of Educational Psychology* 95:409–418.

Mahoney, J.L., and Stattin, H. 2000. Leisure time activities and adolescent anti-social behavior: The role of structure and social context. *Journal of Adolescence* 23:113–127.

Manning, W.D., and Lamb, K. 2003. Adolescent well-being in cohabiting, married, and single-parent families. *Journal of Marriage and Family* 65:876–893.

Margolin, G., and Gordis, E.B. 2000. The effects of family and community violence on children. *Annual Review of Psychology* 51:445–479.

Mason, W.A., Zimmerman, L., and Evans, W. 1998. Sexual and physical abuse among incarcerated youth: Implications for sexual behavior, contraceptive use, and teenage pregnancy. *Child Abuse and Neglect* 22:987–995.

Matsueda, R. 1992. Reflected appraisals, parental labeling, and delinquency: Specifying a symbolic interactionist theory. *American Journal of Sociology* 97:1577–1611.

McBurnett, K., Raine, A., Stouthamer-Loeber, M., Loeber, R., Kumar, A.M., Kumar, M., and Lahey, B.B. 2005. Mood and hormone responses to psychological challenge in adolescent males with conduct problems. *Biological Psychiatry* 57:1109–1116.

McCord, J. 1991. The cycle of crime and socialization practices. *Journal of Criminal Law and Criminology* 82:211–228.

Messner, S.F., Raffalovich, L.E., and McMillan, R. 2001. Economic deprivation and changes in homicide arrest rates for white and black youths, 1967–1998: A national time-series analysis. *Criminology* 39(3):591–613.

Miller, E.M. 1986. *Street Women.* Philadelphia, PA: Temple University Press.

Miller, J., and White, N.A. 2003. Gender and adolescent relationship violence. *Criminology* 41(4):1207–1248.

Moffitt, T.E. 1993. Adolescence-limited and life-course-persistent antisocial behavior: A developmental taxonomy. *Psychological Review* 100:674–701.

Moffitt, T.E., Caspi, A., Belsky, J., and Silva, P.A. 1992. Childhood experience and the onset of menarche: A test of a sociobiological model. *Child Development* 63:47–58.

Moffitt, T.E., Caspi, A., Rutter, M., and Silva, P.A. 2001. *Sex Differences in Antisocial Behavior: Conduct Disorder, Delinquency, and Violence in the Dunedin Longitudinal Study.* New York, NY: Cambridge University Press.

Molnar, B.E., Browne, A., Cerda, M., and Buka, S.L. 2005. Violent behavior by girls reporting violent victimization. *Archives of Pediatric and Adolescent Medicine* 159:731–739.

Morash, M. 1986. Gender, peer group experiences and seriousness of delinquency. *Journal of Research in Crime and Delinquency* 23:43–67.

Obeidallah, D., Brennan, R.T., Brooks-Gunn, J., and Earls, F. 2004. Links between pubertal timing and neighborhood contexts: Implications for girls' violent behavior. *Journal of the American Academy of Child and Adolescent Psychiatry* 43:1460–1468.

Offord, D.R., Boyle, M.H., and Racine, Y. 1989. Ontario Child Health Study: Correlates of Disorder. *Journal of the American Academy of Child and Adolescent Psychiatry* 28:856–860.

Orr, D.P., and Ingersoll, G.M. 1995. The contribution of level of cognitive complexity and pubertal timing to behavioral risk in young adolescents. *Pediatrics* 95:528–533.

Paikoff, R.L., and Brooks-Gunn, J. 1991. Do parent-child relationships change during puberty? *Psychological Bulletin* 110:47–66.

Patterson, G.R., Crosby, L., and Vuchinich, S. 1992. Predicting risk for early police arrest. *Journal of Quantitative Criminology* 8:335–355.

Paulson, M.J., Coombs, R.H., and Richardson, M.A. 1990. School performance, academic aspirations, and drug use among children and adolescents. *Journal of Drug Education* 20(4):289–303.

Payne, A.A., and Gottfredson, D.C. 2005. Gender and race-based outcomes in the effect of school-related factors on delinquency and victimization. Unpublished manuscript.

Pearce, L.D., and Haynie, D.L. 2004. Intergenerational religious dynamics and adolescent delinquency. *Social Forces* 82:1153–1172.

Poe-Yamagata, E., and Butts, J.A. 1996. *Female Offenders in the Juvenile Justice System: Statistics Summary.* Summary. Washington, DC: U.S. Department of Justice, Office of Justice Programs, Office of Juvenile Justice and Delinquency Prevention.

Regnerus, M.D. 2003. Moral communities and adolescent delinquency. *Sociological Quarterly* 44:523–554.

Regnerus, M.D., and Elder, G.H. 2003. Religion and vulnerability among low-risk adolescents. *Social Science Research* 32:633–658.

Rieder, J., and Coupey, S.M. 1999. Update on pubertal development. *Current Opinion in Obstetrics and Gynecology* 11:457–462.

Robertson, R.G., Bankier, R.G., and Schwartz, L. 1987. The female offender: A Canadian study. *Canadian Journal of Psychiatry* 32:749–755.

Rosay, A.B., Gottfredson, D.C., Armstrong, T.A., and Harmon, M.A. 2000. Invariance of measures of prevention program effectiveness: A replication. *Journal of Quantitative Criminology* 16:341–367.

Rowe, D.C., and Farrington, D.P. 1997. The familial transmission of criminal convictions. *Criminology* 35:177–201.

Sale, E., Sambrano, S., Springer, J.F., and Turner, C.W. 2003. Risk, protection, and substance use in adolescents: A multi-site model. *Journal of Drug Education* 33(1): 91–105.

Sampson, R.J., Morenoff, J.D., and Gannon-Rowley, T. 2002. Assessing neighborhood effects: Social processes and new directions in research. *Annual Review of Sociology* 28:443–478.

Satterfield, J.H., and Schell, A. 1997. A prospective study of hyperactive boys with conduct problems and normal boys: Adolescent and adult criminality. *Journal of American Academy of Child and Adolescent Psychiatry* 36:1726–1735.

Schlossman, S., and Cairns, R.B. 1993. Problem girls: Observations on past and present. In *Children in Time and Place: Developmental and Historical Insights,* edited by G.H. Elder Jr., J. Modell, and R.D. Parke. New York, NY: Cambridge University Press, pp. 110–130.

Shelton, D. 2004. Experiences of detained young offenders in need of mental health care. *Journal of Nursing Scholarship* 36:129–133.

Sherkat, D.E., and Ellison, C.G. 1999. Recent developments and current controversies in the sociology of religion. *Annual Review of Sociology* 25:363–394.

Siegel, J.A., and Williams, L.M. 2003. The relationship between child sexual abuse and female delinquency and crime: A prospective study. *Journal of Research in Crime and Delinquency* 40:71–94.

Sinha, R. 2001. How does stress increase risk of drug abuse and relapse? *Psychopharmacology* 158:343–359.

Smith, C. 2005. *Soul Searching: The Religious and Spiritual Lives of American Teenagers.* New York, NY: Oxford University Press.

Smith, C., Faris, R., Denton, M.L., and Regnerus, R. 2003. Mapping American adolescent subjective religiosity and attitudes of alienation toward religion: A research report. *Sociology of Religion* 64:111–133.

Smith, D.K., Leve, L.D., and Chamberlain, P. 2006. Adolescent girls' offending and health-risking sexual behavior: The predictive role of trauma. *Child Maltreatment* 11:346–353.

Snell, T. 1994. *Women in Prison: Survey of State Prison Inmates, 1991.* Special Report. Washington, DC: U.S. Department of Justice, Office of Justice Programs, Bureau of Justice Statistics.

Snyder, H. 2000. *Sexual Assault of Young Children as Reported to Law Enforcement: Victim, Incident, and Offender Characteristics.*

Report. Washington, DC: U.S. Department of Justice, Office of Justice Programs, Bureau of Justice Statistics.

Snyder, H. 2008. *Juvenile Arrests 2006.* Bulletin. Washington, DC: U.S. Department of Justice, Office of Justice Programs, Office of Juvenile Justice and Delinquency Prevention.

Snyder, H., and Sickmund, M. 2006. *Juvenile Offenders and Victims: 2006 National Report.* Washington, DC: U.S. Department of Justice, Office of Justice Programs, Office of Juvenile Justice and Delinquency Prevention.

Song, L.Y., Singer, M.I., and Anglin, T.M. 1998. Violence exposure and emotional trauma as contributors to adolescents' violent behaviors. *Archives of Pediatrics and Adolescent Medicine* 152(6):531–536.

Spohn, R.E. 2000. Gender differences in the effect of child maltreatment on criminal activity over the life course. In *Families, Crime, and Criminal Justice,* Vol. 2, edited by G.L. Fox and M.L. Benson. Stamford, CT: JAI Press, pp. 207–231.

Stark, R., Kent, L., and Doyle, D. 1982. Religion and delinquency: The ecology of a lost relationship. *Journal of Research in Crime and Delinquency* 19:4–24.

Stattin, H., and Magnusson, D. 1989. The role of early aggressive behavior in the frequency, seriousness, and types of later crime. *Journal of Consulting and Clinical Psychology* 57:710–718.

Stattin, H., and Magnusson, D. 1990. *Pubertal Maturation in Female Development, Vol. 2: Paths through Life.* Hillsdale, NJ: Erlbaum.

Steffensmeier, D., and Haynie, D. 2000. Gender, structural disadvantage, and urban crime: Do macro social variables also explain female offending rates? *Criminology* 38(2):403–439.

Steffensmeier, D., Schwartz, J., Zhong, H., and Ackermann, J. 2005. An assessment of recent trends in girls' violence using diverse longitudinal sources: Is the gender gap closing? *Criminology* 43(2):355–406.

Stice, E., Presnell, K., and Bearman, S.K. 2001. Relation of early menarche to depression, eating disorders, substance abuse, and comorbid psychopathology among adolescent girls. *Developmental Psychology* 37:608–619.

Stiffman, A.R. 1989. Physical and sexual abuse in runaway youths. *Child Abuse and Neglect* 13:417–426.

Teplin, L.A., Abram, K.M., McClelland, G.M., Dulcan, M.K., and Mericle, A.A. 2002. Psychiatric disorders in youth in juvenile detention. *Archives of General Psychiatry* 59:1133–1143.

Thornberry, T.P., Esbensen, F.A., and Van Kammen, W.B. 1993. Commitment to school and delinquency. In *Urban Delinquency and Substance Abuse,* edited by D. Huizinga, R. Loeber, and T.P. Thornberry. Washington, DC: U.S. Department of Justice, Office of Justice Programs, Office of Juvenile Justice and Delinquency Prevention, pp. 10/1–10/26.

Thornberry, T.P., Lizotte, A.J., Krohn, M.D., Farnworth, M., and Jang, S.J. 1991. Testing interactional theory: An examination of reciprocal causal relationships among family, school, and delinquency. *Journal of Criminal Law and Criminology* 82(1):3–35.

Warr, M. 1996. Organization and instigation in delinquent groups. *Criminology* 24:11–38.

Warr, M. 2002. *Companions in Crime: The Social Aspects of Criminal Conduct.* New York, NY: Cambridge University Press.

Weichold, K., Silbereisen, R.K., and Schmitt-Rodermund, E. 2003. Short-term and long-term consequences of early versus late physical maturation in adolescents. In *Gender Differences at Puberty,* edited by C. Hayward. New York, NY: Cambridge University Press, pp. 241–276.

Weithorn, L.A. 1988. Mental hospitalization of troublesome youth: An analysis of skyrocketing admission rates. *Stanford Law Review* 40:773–838.

Welsh, L.A., Archambault, F.X., Janus, M.D., and Brown, S.W. 1995. *Running for Their Lives: Physical and Sexual Abuse of Runaway Adolescents.* New York, NY: Garland.

Welsh, W.N., Greene, J.R., and Jenkins, P.H. 1999. School disorder: The influence of individual, institutional, and community factors. *Criminology* 37(1):73–115.

Widom, C.S. 1989a. Child abuse, neglect, and violent criminal behavior. *Criminology* 27:251–272.

Widom, C.S. 1989b. The cycle of violence. *Science* 244:160–166.

Widom, C.S. 1989c. The intergenerational transmission of violence. In *Pathways to Criminal Violence,* edited by N.A. Weiner and M.E. Wolfgang. Newbury Park, CA: Sage Publications, pp. 137–201.

Widom, C.S. 1991. Childhood victimization: Risk factor for delinquency. In *Adolescent Stress: Causes and Consequences,* edited by M.E. Colten and S. Gore. New York, NY: Aldine De Gruyter.

Widom, C.S. 1995. *Victims of Childhood Sexual Abuse: Later Criminal Consequences.* Washington, DC: U.S. Department of Justice, Office of Justice Programs, National Institute of Justice.

Widom, C.S., and Ames, M.A. 1994. Criminal consequences of childhood sexual victimization. *Child Abuse and Neglect* 18:303–318.

Widom, C.S., and Maxfield, M.G. 2001. *An Update on the Cycle of Violence.* Research in Brief. Washington, DC: U.S. Department of Justice, Office of Justice Programs, National Institute of Justice.

Wood, J., Foy, D., Goguen, C., Pynoos, R., and James, C. 2002. Violence exposure and PTSD among delinquent girls. *Journal of Aggression, Maltreatment and Trauma* 6:109–126.

Zweig, J.M., Sayer, A., Crockett, L.J., and Vicary, J.R. 2002. Adolescent risk factors for sexual victimization: A longitudinal analysis of rural women. *Journal of Adolescent Research* 17(6): 586–603.

Acknowledgments

The Girls Study Group is a group of multidisciplinary experts who have been convened to assess current knowledge about the patterns and causes of female delinquency and to design appropriate intervention programs based on this information.

This bulletin was developed by Margaret A. Zahn (Principal Investigator of the Girls Study Group project, 2004–2008) and is based on excerpts from manuscripts written for the Girls Study Group by the following authors:

- Robert Agnew, Professor, Department of Sociology, Emory University.

- Diana Fishbein, Director, Transdisciplinary Behavioral Science Program, RTI International.

- Shari Miller, Research Psychologist, RTI International.

- Donna-Marie Winn, Senior Research Scientist, Center for Social Demography and Ethnography, Duke University.

- Gayle Dakoff, Associate Research Professor, Department of Epidemiology and Public Health, University of Miami.

- Candace Kruttschnitt, Professor, Department of Sociology, University of Toronto.

- Peggy Giordano, Professor of Sociology, Center for Family and Demographic Research, Bowling Green State University.

- Denise C. Gottfredson, Professor, Department of Criminal Justice and Criminology, University of Maryland.

- Allison A. Payne, Assistant Professor, Department of Sociology and Criminal Justice, Villanova University.

- Barry C. Feld, Professor, School of Law, University of Minnesota.

- Meda Chesney-Lind, Professor, Women's Studies Program, University of Hawaii—Manoa.

Full results are available in the book *The Delinquent Girl* published by Temple University Press, January 2009.

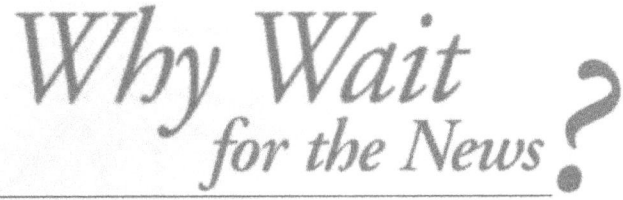

Sign Up for OJJDP's Online Subscriptions

➤ **JUVJUST** e-mails information two to three times per week from OJJDP and the field about new publications, funding opportunities, and upcoming conferences.

➤ **The OJJDP News @ a Glance** bimonthly electronic newsletter covers many of the same topics as JUVJUST—plus recent OJJDP activities—but in more depth.

It's easy: go to OJJDP's home page (www.ojp.usdoj.gov/ojjdp) and click on the "Subscribe" links to JUVJUST and/or OJJDP News @ a Glance.

Office of Juvenile Justice
and Delinquency Prevention

This bulletin was prepared under cooperative agreement number 2004–JF–FX–K001 from the Office of Juvenile Justice and Delinquency Prevention (OJJDP), U.S. Department of Justice.

Points of view or opinions expressed in this document are those of the authors and do not necessarily represent the official position or policies of OJJDP or the U.S. Department of Justice.

The Office of Juvenile Justice and Delinquency Prevention is a component of the Office of Justice Programs, which also includes the Bureau of Justice Assistance; the Bureau of Justice Statistics; the Community Capacity Development Office; the National Institute of Justice; the Office for Victims of Crime; and the Office of Sex Offender Sentencing, Monitoring, Apprehending, Registering, and Tracking (SMART).